HEROD'S CHILDREN CRUMULENT COLLECTION

ROLAND T WOODWARD

DEDICATION

This collection is dedicated to every poet, published or unpublished, who knows the pain

of rejection of their work.

ABOUT THE AUTHOR

Roland Woodward is a retired chartered forensic psychologist. He is dyslexic and lives in the United Kingdom, where he has written poetry all his life. He has now found time to join other poets in his local area and to pursue publishing his poetry. Roland has previously published The Cancer Years: So Far, a collection of poems which were written during his ongoing battle with prostate cancer, which was diagnosed in 2019. He has also published The Travelling Years, a collection of poems written in English hotels and restaurants while traveling as a clinician.

This third short collection, Herod's Children Crumulent Collection, is a collection of his failed poems. They have been submitted and rejected in various competitions and formats, but for which he still harbors a soft spot. Roland hopes that this third poetry collection finds favor with those who have experienced the life of a would-be competition winner or aspire to be a published poet. It seems that rejection is the poet's lot. To survive the critical eye of others and still hold fast to the experience that prompted the urge to write and try and express the individual's experience of the moment seems too precious to be chewed up and spat out and, worst of all, to be cast aside. This collection may have failed in the arena, but each one has a place in Roland's life and experience. He hopes it encourages others to hold onto their urges to write and value that process as a way of making meaning of the world and their internal personal universe.

Acknowledgment

I extend my heartfelt gratitude to WritersClique.com for publishing this book and a special thanks to Adam Smith, my project managers, for their invaluable guidance. My editors, Anne and Shailene, deserve immense appreciation for their meticulous work and dedication. This book is a testament to the collective effort and talent of all involved.

I want to acknowledge all the Dyslexics of the world who have struggled to overcome whatever version of the condition they have. In many cases, Dyslexia has been reframed to embrace the enhancements that it brings. However, many still struggle to be understood. They are not being deliberately difficult, and they are not stupid; they are just struggling with making sense of words and language that others take in their stride. As someone who was once a child doing raffia work at the back of the class while others got on with reading and writing, I hope that this small collection encourages fellow Dyslexics to find their way of expressing their way of making meaning of the world. I want to acknowledge all their struggles and achievements and encourage them to continue.

Finally, I want to acknowledge Homer Simpson for the word Crumulent. My interpretation is that he uses it to value something as useless with disdain. Something I have felt has been applied to some of my work, as I am sure many others have.

TABLE OF CONTENTS

227

THIRD STAIR

Sitting here three stairs up

In the middle of everything

The very heart of the house,

Inside but outside.

From here, the house revolves.

But I never need to enter.

Each single room is a world,

But the house is a universe.

Here, I am amidst it all,

But oh so distant,

A stranger in a family land

Where everything is so intimate

But intangible, unfathomable.

It is the comfort that I seek,

Here, between nexus and zenith

Of belonging.

227

10th January 1989

239

CHARCOAL DRAWING

Charcoal men dangling from street wreckage

Turning slowly above a crowd

Noisy, vengeful men.

The black rigidity of the limbs

The stumpiness of the cut ends

In a star-shape

Hanging.

A pair of charred people

No longer anything other than the basest carbon.

Nothing left to call human

Neither moved by wind nor by passion

Between the dead and the living, only the black element

Holds them in common.

From this to that

In one blinding flash

Humanity degraded in both its forms

Dead or alive.

239 31-01-5.

242

BE MORE INTERESTED.

I meet an old lover and babble.

It's all about me.

Why on earth would anyone stay?

When all I do is me.

No "How are you",

"Where are you now"

"Is life good?"

"Your partner, well."

"Been anywhere nice."

"Tell me your health."

"Are you happy"

"Are you ill?"

I really want to know.

But it comes out to me.

Attachment fuck up me.

If I am only me

It's unimpressive

And Oh, so boring.

No divide between me

And me and me and me.

Do something different

At least, remember.

Old lovers bring home.

My promise always to be a friend

And how is that to be?

It cannot be if it is just me.

And in that lies the seed

Of being boring, avoided

And truly alone,

With only me for company.

Perhaps then I will know

What it feels like to

Have to listen and never

Be asked how I am.

More me

Back to me

Me, me, me.

242

23-03-2005

244

CARO, DAZIEL AND BACON

From megalithic iron to minute wood,

From light and large to dark and small,

The hands that crafted these

Are not idly living lives.

Boxes, huge from sleepers

Like collections boxes of hewn chocolates,

Whilst trumpets herald and draw attention.

In dimness to preserve the engraver's art,

Etched wonders,

Every line of exquisite pages,

Lives in lines, in relief, incredible.

The elephant and ant of art,

Sitting there,

Daring people to notice.

Orange distortion comes

Crashing through the senses

As what is recognisable,

But never conceived invades.

Bodies but not a way of being

Not seen before is

There before, undeniably.

Stunned and once more

An experience to show

That I have no idea.

I do not understand.

I do not know.

The mystery is still.

As redraw.

Outside and breathless

I wonder why I do this thing,

When others are so much surer

In their unknowing and

The exploration.

244

18-03-05

After a visit to the Tate Gallery on the 17th March 05.

Written at the Elevertham Hotel.

252

OH, HOW?

So how can it come to this?

Hurt and yet loving,

The bond that ties the daughter to the mother

Twisted, stretched, and contorted yet unyielding.

Though one end is fixed fast

Whilst the other lashes around in the tempest,

Still, it passes for love.

No flow of rich nutrients from the mother to her baby

But how the child cries out for rich blood,

Rich blood of kin, blood in the line,

Long and keening the voice in the wilderness,

Blood with the oxygen of love in it.

Bereft of mother,

Never noticed,

Pain ignored.

Loss and rape carved deep,

All in vain as blind eyes and shriveled soul,

Avert themselves unable to acknowledge.

The single most solitaire being left,

Huddled in the sea of the desert,

Washed with shame and guilt,

Tortured with the imagined evil within,

Sanity ragged and tattered, flapping in the breeze,

A small and urgent hand clutching the sand,

And like the mother, the sand declines the grasp.

Does nothing in this barrenness touch the cord?

What lightness of being, what delicate balance,

The flow of time bends itself around her,

Trying to do no further harm,

Avoiding the scars of old,

Almost apologising for its old indifference.

If ever a voice was raised that held in it such need

I never heard it,

This cry deafens me,

Why cannot her own flesh bear witness to its own progeny?

24th November 2005

(At Windsor)

253

STRETCH MARKS OF THE SOUL

Orange oil gentled in the artwork of despair,

 a preparation of the body to be held,

Eyes that meet and hold the moment,

That instant in which the warm wave

Breaks upon the shores of thawing life,

When life stirs in the marrow of the bone,

So nearly cut through the muscle and skin.

The protective barrier against the world,

Breached only by the impulse to release the imagined,

The fantasy monster concocted inside.

Deep in its caves of conscience,

Thrust there by beast beloved,

But betrayer of the trust, the love.

Wrecked innocence, trashed and despoiled,

Left to totter from one painful way

To another torturous path, aching,

Bleeding and pleading for respite,

Crying out for peace and rest.

Yet all the time, relentlessly alive and striving,

Becoming, waiting like the winter-hardened seed.

Artwork of the highest order,

A human pain of life,

The struggle to live,

To love and to belong.

Connected to the world,

The natural force to grow,

To know what it is to have a body whole,

A mind to appreciate it,

And to be.

A place, a person in the world,

Bearing the stretch marks of the soul

Born and flourishing.

253

29th NOVEMBER 2005

14

265

ST PANCREAS

So where did it go

That kick your legs,

Wave your arms,

That baby spontaneity.

Quick as a flash

A windmill of pink

As little arms and legs

Wave like an upturned turtle.

Just because it could,

Just because it is now.

A flash of life amidst the

trudging army of grimness

Passing through, traveling on,

All about the business of life.

That tide of impenetrable greyness

That adulthood joins.

Purposeful disillusionment is making its way.

Going nowhere except further away.

Only a baby can light up the gloom

With a single bolt of life,

Waving at Mother,

Just because.

Where Oh where is my baby spark?

Am I really sunk in this big person?

In an instant

Life as it comes, fresh

And dazzling.

265

16th May 2007

274

A PLACE FOR FRIENDLY DEAD ATHEISTS

Over there in the dark corner

Next to the anarchists,

Is that where it is?

That place where friendly dead atheists go.

What do you do with the non-believers?

The faithless but kindly folk.

Never hurt a fly, and compassionate to others.

Straightforward and honest

And now a conundrum.

For the life of them, they just could not,

Would not go beyond the evidence,

The logic, the facts.

Faithlessness is their only fault.

To be weighed on the scales and found to be light.

The leap, the bound into ignorance and blindness

This is what they would not do.

All that good was done because people

Are people, so why wouldn't you?

People were enough in themselves,

There was no need for doing good

Or anyone's work or a deity's bidding.

In fact, ` there was just doing.

Of course, the vested interests will

Claim mystical and guided ways,

But what else can they do?

Faced with ordinary and real magic

The magicians, necromancers, and illusionists

Know themselves laid bare.

Only then do they crumble and descend

The darker path to destroy what

Points to the sleight of hand or mind.

So now condemned the friendly atheist

Stands accused of denial and arrogance.

How else can they be what they are,

It's clear that they are evil,

The explanation of the ignorant,

Intellectually lazy and superstitious

And so it is complete and the right

Minded status quo prevails.

And kindness, for kindness's sake, dies.

A little more. And between us

The distance grows. And our imagined

Meaning draws further from ourselves.

That's me in the corner

Losing my humanity.

274

Between 23rd and 27th October 2008.

277

ARTISTS NOTE

Mish cried in the face of

Care, a struggler fighting

Hard to play faithfully the

Life that being had dealt

Her.

The highs, the lows and

The old solutions now the

Problem. Love is not enough,

No, that's not right; love is

Enough, sex is not. How

Hard that adolescent

Longing lingers.

277 11th August 2009

The Davenport Hotel

285

It's not so much the blades

or the cuts,

not even the thickness of the blood,

but it is the despair.

Knowing the forces behind the act,

the loss of self in the chaos,

a world so cruel and demanding

that only the gift of flesh will do.

It is not just the real thing

but the seeping wound when there is another.

Perhaps not even that, but the knowing

that whatever you do makes no difference.

That wanting another is there,

there and hidden and denied.

Trying to confront it, the truth

does fuck all good.

It just goes deeper and lives underground.

It becomes nameless,

Invisible.

And inside part of me dies.

There's none left now,

just the perception of deception,

being taken for a fool.

The convenient port of call that provides shelter,

while the pirate sport on the sea.

Whatever was is no more.

It is only a matter of time before the shipwreck.

285

8th March 2010

286

Empty seats, empty hall

stalls of stalwarts

and a man and his art.

Words to inspire, no,

words to make you laugh,

except the room is cold,

the themes old, stories told

so aged, creeping up a slow death.

Surprise me!

Go on!

Show me something new,

Make me laugh.

286

(York Opera House. 2011 Jerry Sadowitz)

287

My 50th birthday present to you

could have been a book that would have been safe,

smellies are always tricky, and chocolate is out.

Music and film are good for strangers, you're not.

I thought of finding words of wisdom,

consolation of growing wise with experience,

an aphorism to sum it all up,

but all trite and bland.

Jewellery, bright shiny thing, inappropriate, too much explanation.

So what then do I give you to mark your fifty?

Typically, my mind presents the surreal;

An embroidered nose bag for Mollie

hand-crafted necklaces for dogs, and matching rain boots, too.

All, of course, a diversion.

What to give the mischievous woman who sees films alone?

It's a mystery,

other than there is a friend who thinks of you,

wants to find the right thing

and hopes that being thought off is enough.

Happy birthday.

287

25th January 2012

288

Adelle in my ears

on a laptop

in my bed

alone again.

Of all the things

I miss to do

is listening.

Alone again.

writing a poem again,

in a room,

with therapy around.

Alone, again.

An interlude

288 11th April 2012

Tuke Centre Room 4. York

295

DUCKLINGS AT SWINFEN

In the midst of wire, ducklings

following their mother

across a pond of tarmac.

Hunched ducks dotted around,

not paddling, not swimming, sitting.

No water to be seen, just black stuff

rimmed by trodden green.

Dependent, hurrying bundles, staying close,

amongst the lost boys,

and their guards.

This all taken as a matter of fact,

to me, a wonder.

In all the places to find

new life in such an array

this was the last place,

that scuttling, piping, urgency of survival

and dependency.

Yet mother chooses prison.

To bring her children

to safety and to life.

Astounding, but ignored.

That's prison for you.

295

Ducklings observed when visiting HMP Swinfen Hall 15th April 2014

299

Fat arseholes,

that mixed couple

gross and spread

across four first class.

The rattle of their prattle

mechanical and greased.

The assumption of space

including strewn bags,

unable to raise their arms

under the weight of

abdominal aprons,

to put the stowables

in the racks provided.

Hideous, purpoid love

ordering take away

via mobile app.

Raucously, rapaciously

declaring humanities

obesity without a hint

of awareness.

But it wants electricity.

For its toys.

It's narcissistic needs.

to be fed with something

and like a baby

wails when thwarted.

The snack trolley is doomed.

299 9th May 2014

Fat people on a train journey from London.

301

It's so naughty

that smooth cheek

proffered and kissed

in a formal farewell.

A big surprise

the warmth of youth.

So unexpected,

not the "nice to meet you."

"See you," "Take care,"

wave goodbye moment

that was expected.

A spontaneous moment

Still, after all these years

of talk and touch

the family's icy distance

and the lack of touch

make such moments perilous.

What for others is normal,

easy, expected, done

is, for me, a minefield,

never knowing when or how

but more precarious...

What might be felt?

The shock of all that

could be

Amidst the realisation

that this convention

is a mirror for my

own delusions and failings.

No one wants this,

this man of age

full of vulnerabilities,

confusion and errors.

This social nicety picks out

the lingering desires

and the lost time

alongside what others

must surely construct me as

in their heads.

As...

301 14th May 2014

An end to a meeting with C and the interrupted thoughts that followed.

306

C34A

They sold me a seat

C34A

I board the train to

C34A

And walk the aisle to

C34A

To find that they sold me a luggage rack at

C34A

Says it all.

C34A.

306 21st November 2014

Train Journey from Leicester to St Pancras

310

Biffa Bin Boy me,

none of your Barnardo's boy,

that was luxury

Biffa Bin Boy knows collection day

No metal chewing for this one.

Biffa Bin Boy is brighter than the average

Solid roof and walls from wind and rain.

No god stuff and charity, poor boy

Biffa Bin Boy is free.

310 Premier Inn Pity Me, Durham

19th May 2015

35

319

Running, dribbling man,

a madness high-pitched

contained by soft hands.

Another world lived out

amidst the dour closet

full of moths.

Running dribbling man

A husband, father, son

all come to this.

Mindlessness, being consumed.

A brain no longer working.

Confined, atrophied, starved,

a beastly end.

Running dribbling man

Wide-eyed and panicked,

no words to tell,

no vocabulary left

only an impulse to the unseen,

not knowing why or how.

Running dribbling, man.

There is no deep meaning,

no strange wisdom

this is Man at his end

already dead and waiting

for the body to follow suit.

Still and dry

319 9th May 2017

Premier Inn, Hull

After a visit to a Hospital.

320

I am on a train,

It's infested.

The clicking of the techno beetle

rattles along.

It's in the seats,

the overheads and racks.

A vast army of gnawing anxiety

being anywhere but on the train.

One lone watcher

seven tapers staring twelve inches

being anywhere but not here.

And on goes the clicking

the chewing away at the fabric

and the sucking at their souls.

All unconnected

as WiFi sucks them in,

draws out their lives

and spills it into the void.

Lost in space with their money,

their "friends," their likes,

lusts.

It is a public life that is machined,

electronic extensions of something beyond

eight o'clock and fully lost

Old bloke in the corner

watch saying "now."

And he smiles.

320 24th May 2017 Premier Inn Thetford

After a train trip to London EEL meeting.

321

Oh dismal day,

amateurs and fools

but the good will prevail.

Little piggy brain

and little piggy belly

trots big-mouthed

but small-minded

embarrassed by the pretense,

by the effrontery

to pretend to know.

A bully through and through,

clip clop go the trotters

across a lino hallway,

the old dying all around.

321 6th June 2017

A Hospital visit.

324

Do you regret the wolves?

That inked reminder?

The girl on the swing

bold and coloured

illuminates the back,

and the then back

there.

324 Windermere House

31-07-2017

325

Fucking envelopes, or lack of them

rules the world. No envelopes

no survey, no letter, no responses,

it just accentuates being alone,

out of mind, out of other's minds,

no idea how desperate you are.

I like to think I'm lucky,

a good person with a good heart

but not what makes me feel the animal.

No "getting the marmosets out,"

Virginia knows what that means,

and even as she drowns

she leaves a perfect marriage.

This is the difficult bit,

this is what proves my humanity,

this is the test

and I still fear to fail,

having failed myself a million times

over.

325 Windermere House 31-07-2017

326

I had forgotten Ginsberg

until Kate reminded me,

"America, I am putting my

Queer shoulder to the wheel."

so ahead, so open, so against,

the KKK USA

where niggers and queers

we're run out of towns

stayed white by fear.

The negro green book of travel

to steer the traveling black

clear of fear and to a bed,

a safe black bed

where the whites avoided

a sort of de-human zoo.

Gay and saying poetry

at festivals, on a step ladder.

I found him uplifting.

Never sure why

but now, in Missouri and York

show me how it is today.

The world's not right

how can I stop?

326   February 2018

After reading about the green book of negro travel.

328

No swimwear,

no list, you see

when juggling

a loss of gravity.

Long preparation

doesn't reach the destination,

anticipation drives and

London sucks at life.

Restless, showered and wined

in sun that glistens

on taxi cabs and glass,

poverty and a get-by class.

Here, rap passes as poetry

without the energy or voice

of a roaring, howling Ginsberg.

328 London 24th April 2018.

336

Dumb with rage

I need to stop,

too much at Home

needs seeing to.

Almost overwhelming,

my teeth grind,

my gear low,

but always forward.

I'm back,

back in the Chinese box.

Normally, I write,

I write a way out

but I am dumb

of mouth and hand

so sit and calm

the inner Dark.

It is here,

my strength,

my gems,

the anvil of

my Forefathers.

the ironwork

of being.

336

20th April 2022.

A15

O.W.B.

Invisible

like a retiring

colleague,

a ghost before gone.

not considered,

a non-contributor

stripped of significance

and worth.

Gone fatherhood,

partnered out,

convicted

sentenced

condemned

to carry the sins

of the tribe

into the wilderness.

There will be no careers,

those are only for

the sorority members

and they made baby

by infirmity.

This is how new

power devours

the old.

A15

Arvon Course 18/11/2021

Note: O.W.B is Old White Bloke

A16

PLIERS AND A MAN

I am steel,

forged in fire,

hammered hard

and tempered.

Plunged in water

hissing steamy anger

at the loss of flame.

There on the anvil

I was malleable,

fashionable,

at the mercy

of the Blacksmith's art.

These are things

my Grandfather forged.

Ironworker,

builder of cars

till war took him

to fight in other lands.

Returning to a "a land for heroes,"

with no work,

and so he gardened,

grew things at Kew

until they fitted an

iron leg.

Forged in fire,

hammered hard

and tempered.

A16 Totleigh 1st Exercise

16/November/2021

A24

You're the sort of bloke

that would run up to me

and shout;

I am the head of my house,

this land is mine

all the way to the river.

My wives are many

my children more.

I slew a Hippo

and wear its teeth

at my throat.

I reply;

I once got a cycling

proficiency badge.

This is what happens

when Africa meets

an Old White Bloke.

Inside, I'm thinking: Empire!

A24 *ARVON* 19/11/2021

Printed in Great Britain
by Amazon